T0194878

WHEN MANDRAKES DON'T WORK

Confronting the challenges of becoming pregnant and having your baby.

MALCOLM O'DEAN

WESTBOW
PRESS®
A DIVISION OF THOMAS NELSON
& ZONDERVAN

WestBow Press books may be ordered through booksellers or by contacting:

WestBow Press
A Division of Thomas Nelson & Zondervan
1663 Liberty Drive
Bloomington, IN 47403
www.westbowpress.com
844-714-3454

ISBN: 978-1-6642-5418-3 (sc)
ISBN: 978-1-6642-5419-0 (hc)
ISBN: 978-1-6642-5417-6 (e)

Library of Congress Control Number: 2021925689

Print information available on the last page.

WestBow Press rev. date: 03/29/2022

DEDICATION

To my unique wife, Shane:

Your quiet speech has been the hallmark of refinement. Your deportment is still a reflection of your intellect. Your first impression on me left a lasting aftereffect. When your faith embraced God's forecast About the childless woman in Psalm 113:9, our relationship rose to a new dimension.

Your faith encounter motivated this written production.

I love you more today than yesterday,

But only half as much as tomorrow.

CONTENTS

PREFACE

IT WAS BY God's grace alone that years of intense desire for a baby blossomed into immeasurable satisfaction and unbridled enjoyment. However, while basking in the comfort of fatherhood, I was awakened to the realization that there are thousands of other human beings whose desire for a baby has not yet been satisfied. Maybe sharing my story would bring some encouragement to them. Then procrastination held me captive from telling the world what God had done for me. Nevertheless, God used the constant reminder of my wife's faith and the bold suggestion of our friend Madeia to deliver me from the chains of procrastination. Consequently, the unheard cries of those who are still craving for their baby energized me to do something.

I am a natural sympathizer with the less fortunate, the *underdog*. I am impassioned to fight for their cause. Therefore, an I-must-do-something-quickly attitude seized me, and I began writing. My passion for advocating on behalf of the underdog intensified when the mother of a newly married couple approached me about their baby plight, which was like the one that I had encountered. At that time, the stakes became even higher. How many others are going through life in that perplexing struggle? That question was answered when a Nigerian Movie called *Baby Blues* was released on YouTube. The movie highlighted the "summit of all fears" when trying to have a baby: an interfering mother and a meddling mother-in-law encapsulated in the same human body. *Baby Blues* epitomized the ceaseless efforts made and the myriad of challenges experienced by so many people just to conceive and give birth to a live and healthy baby.

From that moment, it became a sprint to the finish line. My passion was intensified to get my fellow humans across the gulf of childlessness, up the homestretch of Baby Express, and across the finish line of motherhood and fatherhood. It was like Usain Bolt going around the final curve of a 200-meter sprint and driving up the last 100 meters of the track to another world-record performance. It was as Secretariat galloping down the homestretch at Churchill Downs towards the finish line at the Kentucky Derby. I locked in on the words of Psalm 51:13–14 (KJV): "Then will I teach transgressors thy ways; and sinners shall be converted unto thee. Deliver me from bloodguiltiness, O God, thou God of my salvation: and my tongue shall sing aloud of thy righteousness."

God had delivered me from childlessness, and now my pen must broadcast of his righteousness. Like King David, I must now tell others of God's ways, and assuredly, childless men and women would be converted to mothers and fathers. It was high time for *When Mandrakes Don't Work*.

ACKNOWLEDGMENTS

For my wife, Shane O'Dean:

Thank you for persevering in that God-inspired quest for your baby despite the failed natural and artificial measures that we attempted. I am deeply indebted to your faith, demonstrated by making preparation for your baby even before there was any evidence of pregnancy. I will forever cherish the radiant look of relief and satisfaction that brightened your face as you rediscovered why you were having a second baby. Moreover, I am grateful for your selfless act of grace by granting me permission to publicly share a very personal, private experience with the world.

For my son (Nse), and my daughter (Ariel):

Thank you for being the continual, tangible, living blessings from God to your mother and I from conception; through pregnancy, birth, infancy, and adolescence; to maturity, manliness, and grown-upness. You have consistently enriched our lives with happiness. With all the fatherly kindness and gratitude, I deeply appreciate your patience with me during the numerous occasions when I privately recounted to you The Story (about the circumstances that resulted in your conception). Thanks in advance for your kind indulgence in accommodating me one more time as I share your story publicly.

For our sister in Christ, Madeia:
Thank you for allowing God to make you His public confirmation about our private blessing of a baby, which was secretly granted to us. As we reminisced that experience many years later, you firmly suggested, "Malcolm, I think you should write a book about your experience."

That simple suggestion was another spark of inspiration that reignited a fiery desire in me to write. The conviction with which those words were spoken impressed me that God was again saying something to me through you. Therefore, I did not want to disappoint you, and I would not knowingly disobey God.

For our beloved, deceased parents: Cecil (Doc), Emanuel O'Dean and Evelyn (Pun), Doreen O'Dean; Harold Bender (Uncle Harold) and Bernice Bender (B).
Shane and I are indebted to our loving and steadfast parents. They gave us the awesome foundation of a family full of siblings. This unspoken legacy is what bestowed upon us the unquenchable expectation that we would one day be

parents. As a result, we developed the tenacity needed to take us through that temporary period of aspiring for and anticipating parenthood.

For parents who have adopted:
Selflessly, you have either publicly adopted several children or privately sponsored and supported numerous others. So, whether you continue living in cheerful expectation of your baby or you have settled into the reluctant acceptance of that unwelcomed reality, I applaud your generosity. Continue living with grace and dignity. You are one of God's special gifts to humanity.

For my adopted children,
In 1977, while teaching my first Sunday School class at St. Martin's Anglican Church, I became overwhelmed by the reality that I was now responsible for the lives of other children. Although seventeen years old at that time, I was just another teenager who was high on hormones. In that moment, I realized that something more was needed from me to care for the little ones placed in my charge, something more than being a big brother. So, I committed myself to the task and agreed to this new responsibility if God would help me.

As fatherly concerns and attitudes developed, I adopted the little ones as if they were my own children. After my teaching career began in 1978, all my students became my children.

From Charlestown Secondary School in Georgetown, Guyana, to Tutorial Academy and Berbice High School in New Amsterdam, Guyana. From the teachers at the In-Service Teacher Training Program in New Amsterdam and all the General Educational Development (GED) students at Community College of Philadelphia in Pennsylvania, USA, I inherited adult children. Teaching them Science, Math, or English was as enjoyable as helping one's own baby in taking those first steps. As the Advent Youth Society (AYS) Leader of the Philadelphia and Mizpah Seventh Day Adventist (SDA) churches, respectively, I adopted many more children. As an ordained Elder of the Church, I adopted all the members of the Philadelphia, Eden, Mizpah, and Ephesus SDA churches into my fatherly care. Although happily married when I began serving as an Elder, our marriage had not yet given rise to any children of our own. You all became my children. Therefore, thank you all for affording me the privilege of obtaining eighteen years of training as an apprentice father to you. I will always cherish our times together, as God molded and fashioned me into readiness before blessing my wife and I with children. Without you, I might not have been made ready. This book might not have been inspired, and my gratitude to you might have gone unexpressed. From the bottom of my heart, I express my deepest gratitude in acknowledgement of you. Thank you.

To the Universal Godhead (Father, Creator and Redeemer, Holy Spirit):

Father in heaven, I still don't understand how you can cause cows that are variously colored to eat green grass, drink colorless water, and still produce white milk. Nevertheless, I must acknowledge your providence in taking a girl (who never knew her mother) and a boy (who at 12 years old had lost his father) and cemented their lives together. I marvel how you honored them ten times as mother and father. After losing their stillborn baby, you comforted them with another baby—that baby was me. After longing for many years without a baby, you comforted my wife and I twice, each time with a special baby. Thank you for first granting me as a comfort baby to my parents and later comforting me twice with two unique babies.

INTRODUCTION

PEOPLE SHOULD NOT have to go through life thinking that it's impossible to have their baby. Medical challenges and myriad other circumstances might make their chances improbable. Nevertheless, with God, all things are possible. My wife and I pursued that possibility and were blessed with our babies.

It has been more than twenty years since the last baby. During that time, we have encountered many people who are yet to have their baby. However, a few of the people like us, who found themselves in the same childless circumstance and heard our story, have since gotten their babies. One newly married, young couple that we met have been doubly blessed with two babies. As a result, I have adopted the following words of a well-known song as my motivational platform:

> If I can help somebody as I pass along,
> If I can cheer somebody with a word or song,

If I can spread love's message that the Master
taught,
Then my living shall not be in vain!

So, if I can help some childless couple as I pass along; if I can cheer up one barren woman/man with a word or song; then I must say that the Lord is my Strength and my Song. He is my Baby Supplier and my salvation.

People from every walk of life would always have something to say about having children. However, it does not matter what others are saying. Remember that God already has stated how especially important children are to Him and His Kingdom.

Psalm 127:3 states:

Children are a heritage of the Lord, and the fruit of the womb is his reward. (King James Version, henceforth KJV)

Children are a gift from the LORD; they are a reward from him. (New Living Translation, henceforth NLT)

In every country, language base, culture, and ethnicity, people thank God for their new baby. In doing so, they continually acknowledge God as their Baby Giver. Wess Stafford, president emeritus of Compassion International, must have been convinced about that when he stated, "Every child you encounter is a divine appointment." In Matthew 18:3–4, Jesus stated,

> Verily I say unto you, except ye be converted, and become as little children, ye shall not enter into the kingdom of heaven. Whosoever therefore shall humble himself as this little child, the same is greatest in the kingdom of heaven." (KJV)

> I tell you the truth, unless you turn from your sins and become like little children, you will never get into the Kingdom of Heaven. So anyone who becomes as humble as this little child is the greatest in the Kingdom of Heaven. (NLT)

Hence, the humility of childlikeness is required for adoption into the Kingdom of Heaven. Children are, therefore, living object lessons used by God to teach the world about true surrender and total dependence. It is my personal desire that all childless families be encouraged to pursue their baby by trusting God's will for them. Furthermore, I am optimistic that the combined effect of the shared experiences will ignite or rekindle the quest for your baby.

CHAPTER 1

The Urgent Quest for Mandrakes

SOME PEOPLE ADOPT, but adoption is not an option for many people. Others continue trying as best they know how to fulfill that lifelong desire, yet to no avail. Many have even accepted the fate that pregnancy will not happen for them and have given up all hope. Nevertheless, determined ones relentlessly pursue this apparently elusive goal while clinging tenaciously to the minutest sliver of possibility that it will happen for them. It is said that necessity is the mother of invention. Therefore, the adventurous and creative have resorted to unconventional and extraordinary measures to have a baby. For our heart-to-heart encounter, whether those measures are usual or unusual, common, or uncommon,

1

literal, or figurative, let us cordially agree to refer to all those baby-making measures as *mandrakes*.

In passing, though, I must briefly tell what a literal mandrake is. From a botanical standpoint, a mandrake (*Mandragora officinarum*) is one of the most famous plants known to humanity. The name mandrake refers to a group of about six species of plants in the nightshade family, which are native to the Mediterranean region and the Himalayas. This mandrake is a plant with blue flowers in the winter and yellow plum-like fruit in the summer. Mandrake plants are particularly noted for their potent roots. The shape of the mandrake root has a slight resemblance to the physical form of the human body and has been used in religious and superstitious practices. Mandrakes are even mentioned twice in the Holy Bible, in Genesis 30:14–16 and Song of Solomon 7:13. On both occasions, its biblical use is generally attributed to its supposed fertility power. Mandrakes had become highly prized in many cultures because of the belief that it was an aphrodisiac and promoted fertility. As a result, these perceived qualities, coupled with the fact that these plants were only rarely found in Padanaram, where Leah and Rachel lived (Genesis 28:5), might accurately explain why both sisters intensely craved the mandrakes.

CHAPTER 2

Making a Deal with Mandrakes— Rachel and Leah

LET'S PICK UP the drama in this real-life biblical soap opera which, I have intentionally called *The Days of Jacob's Wives*. You may notice it rhymes with the Daytime Emmy Award–winning and globally renowned soap opera *Days of Our Lives*. After many years of competing for the love and attention of their shared husband, Jacob, the sisters (Leah and Rachel) reached up in a head-on collision. Leah; her servant girl, Zilpah; and Bilhah, Rachel's servant girl, had all borne children for Jacob. Only Rachel remained childless up to that time in this real-life drama. Moreover, Leah had also become temporarily infertile (Genesis 29:31–30:13). Consequently, these rival sisters had been seeking a fertility cure in the mandrake. Rachel, barren until then, more urgently and desperately wanted to try the mandrakes in an attempt to conceive. Therefore, when Leah's son, Rueben, was returning home from the wheat field and Rachel saw that he was carrying mandrakes to his mother, Rachel promptly asked Leah for a portion of her son's mandrakes. Collision! It would have been the normal thing for any caring woman to be concerned about another woman's desire for conception, much more her own sister. However, in Rachel, Leah saw only rivalry and contention. Leah's thoughts appeared to be - *I'm not helping your childless situation*. Leah's exact words were, "Is it a small matter that thou hast taken my husband? and wouldest thou take away my son's mandrakes also?" (Genesis 30:15, KJV).

That is Old English, so let me suggest an updated, paraphrased rendering of Leah's words to Rachel - "So, it was not enough for you to take my husband? Now you also have the nerve to ask for my son's mandrakes?"

Better yet, I have imagined Leah looking Rachel straight in the eye and saying, "You stole my man, right? Now you want me to help you get pregnant by the same man?" I have imagined her feisty attitude, neck movement, hand tattooing the air and ending in a stance and body posture that said, "It's not happening; not over my dead body."

Rachel counterpunched with a proposition in the form of a deal. "How about this? Although it is my turn to have

Jacob in my bed tonight, you can have him to yourself all night in exchange for some of the mandrakes." Solution! Without hesitation, Leah agreed to the terms of Rachel's proposition. They sealed the deal and Rachel got the much-prized mandrakes (fertility herb/aphrodisiac). Leah must have said in her mind, *"Honey, you need more than the mandrakes. You need the man and the mandrakes. I have both."* Listen to exactly how the Bible recorded this episode in *The Days of Jacob's Wives.*

> And Reuben went in the days of wheat harvest, and found mandrakes in the field, and brought them unto his mother Leah. Then Rachel said to Leah, give me, I pray thee, of thy son's mandrakes. And she said unto her, Is it a small matter that thou hast taken my husband? and wouldest thou take away my son's mandrakes also? And Rachel said, Therefore he shall lie with thee to night for thy son's mandrakes. And Jacob came out of the field in the evening, and Leah went out to meet him, and said, Thou must come in unto me; for surely I have hired thee with my son's mandrakes. And he lay with her that night. (Genesis 30:14–16, KJV; emphasis added)

Nevertheless, despite Rachel's later use of the mandrakes, they did not produce the expected result of conception. My goodness! What do you do when your mandrakes don't work? When you've tried various conjugal positions, different times of the day, feng shui, black cohosh, ashwagandha, capadulla, maca, moringa, sarsaparilla, licorice, locust bark, yohimbe, and rounds of in vitro fertilization but still no pregnancy? Where do you turn, and who do you turn to? Rachel turned to her husband Jacob with the ultimatum, "Give me children or else I'll die" (Genesis 30:1, KJV). Wow! He was in trouble on an island all by himself. That island I know. Reluctantly, I once occupied that island. I stood there like a banished buccaneer because I did not bring home the expected treasure (a baby). Here is a worthy, timely reminder: although men actively participate in the act of copulation, they have absolutely no control over conception. Therefore, Jacob responded with the question, "Am I in God's stead, who hath withheld from thee the fruit of the womb?" (Genesis 30:2, KJV).

Sometime after Rachel had made a deal for mandrakes with Leah, God remembered Rachel, and she conceived her first child (Genesis 30:22). Later, I'll explain what "God remembered Rachel" really means. After Rachel's mandrakes failed, God's intervention stimulated Rachel's conception. You see, it was because of hatred toward Leah that God had made Rachel barren. "And when the Lord saw that Leah was hated, he opened her womb: but Rachel was barren" (Genesis 29:31, KJV). God was the reason why Rachel could not conceive a baby, and God was the reason why she subsequently conceived two babies, Joseph and Benjamin. Therefore, like Rachel, I urge you to turn to God when your mandrakes don't work. First, turn to Him in acknowledgment of and in confession for any unkind desire or thought toward another person. As He did with Rachel, He can heal your mind of all unwholesome feelings toward others and heal your childless situation. It is apt to remind you at this point in our heart-to-heart discourse that God does not hear the prayers of anyone who harbors ill feelings toward another person.

If I regard iniquity in my heart, the Lord will not hear me. (Psalm 66:18, KJV)

In some situations, mandrakes do not work for any woman because of the toxic pollution of the immediate physical environment. This was the case recorded in the Bible about the surrounding environment of a place called Jericho.

CHAPTER 3

Death in the Water— Miscarriages at Jericho

MANY YEARS BEFORE the current environmental crisis, God had destroyed the original Canaanite city of Jericho. God had also informed the Hebrews, through Joshua, that the city of Jericho should not be rebuilt (Joshua 6:20–26). More than one hundred years later, after the death of King Solomon and after the kingdom of David had been divided into the Northern division (Israel) and the Southern division (Judah), no one had tried to rebuild the city of Jericho. However, during the reign of King Ahab, when Israel openly rebelled against God, Hiel rebuilt the city of Jericho. He did this at the cost of his firstborn, Abiram, and his youngest son, Segub (1 Kings 16:34), just as Joshua had said. It is in this rebuilt modern city of Jericho that Elisha the prophet lived immediately after Elijah had been translated to heaven. Shortly after Elisha settled down in Jericho, a party of fifty men returned from their unsuccessful three-day search for Elijah, because they had disbelieved Elisha's eyewitness report that Elijah had been taken up to heaven. Then residents of the rebuilt modern Jericho approached Elisha and complained about the polluted water and the barrenness of the land.

> And when they came again to him ("for he tarried at Jericho") he said unto them, Did I not say unto you, Go not? And the men of the city said unto Elisha, Behold, I pray thee, the situation of this city is pleasant, as my lord seeth: but *the water is naught, and the ground barren.* And he said, Bring me a new cruse, and put salt therein. And they brought it to him. And he went forth unto the spring of the waters, and cast the salt in there, and said, Thus saith the LORD, *I have healed these waters; there shall not be from thence any more death or barren land.* So the waters were healed unto this day, according to the saying of Elisha which he spake. (2 Kings 2:18–22, KJV; *emphasis added*)

10

"The water is naught" literally means "the water is bad." Updated to present-day English, "the water is bad" indicates that the water was polluted. Now that's a problem for both human life and livestock. What compounded this seriously grave environmental hazard is the statement that followed "the water is naught" (i.e., "and the ground barren.") The Hebrew word *shakol* (shaw-kole), from which the English word "barren" is translated literally means to miscarry (i.e., to suffer abortion); to cast calf; to make childless; to rob of children.

Now, let us put it all together. "The water is naught, and the ground barren" simply means that because of the polluted water, man, and animals (livestock) suffered miscarriages. Miscarriages have become very sensitive occurrences to medical practitioners and utterly despised events to many prospective parents. One moment you are basking in the unique experience of carrying another human life that has become a part of you. Then some mysterious situation occurs that shatters all your dreams and aspirations for your precious "baby." "Devastating," "disastrous," and "traumatic" are just a few adjectives to describe this stealthy baby-snatcher. Let me publicly acknowledge the unsurpassed pain experienced by all the parents (especially mothers) who have been ambushed and robbed by this "prenatal burglar," better known as "miscarriage." It takes all one's strength, determination, hope and tenacity to fight through this prenatal tsunami (tidal wave) caused by the seismic tremor (earthquake) of death.

You must fight like the Nunez baby, along with thirty-nine other newborn babies and infants, who survived the twin earthquakes that rocked Mexico City on September 19 and 20 of 1985. (*New York Times,* section A, page 2, October 16, 1985; and the *Chicago Tribune,* September 28, 1985, "'Miracle Babies' Survive Quake"). Those babies became known to the world as the 'Miracle Babies of Mexico City'. Their fight, amidst the agents of destruction and death, was simply to trust in and depend completely on someone else for deliverance. That is called the *fight of faith.*

Fight like that fifteen-day-old baby girl found alive in a crumbled house, after she had spent nearly half her life without food or water amid the ruins of the massive earthquake in Haiti on Tuesday, January 12, 2010. See the Article titled "A Week After Earthquake, 15-Day-Old Baby Found Alive" *by Christopher Rhoads and Michael M. Phillips* (Wall Street Journal, January 20, 2010, 7:47 pm ET). The 2010 Haiti disaster was a 7.0-magnitude earthquake with an epicenter just 16 miles away from the capital of Port-au-Prince. The tremor was felt as far away as Cuba and Venezuela. Eight aftershocks followed the same day, and at least fifty-two were recorded over the next two weeks. Despite the tremendous shaking by the earthquake, followed by the constant reverberation of eight aftershocks, the rescue team found the baby in the same bed where she was napping when the earthquake struck. The bed had fallen to the ground floor, but the baby was not even injured. "It was the mercy of God," said her twenty-two-year-old mother, Ms. Joassaint, as she sat breastfeeding her daughter on a makeshift hospital bed next to the heavily damaged city hospital. I believe the testimony of that twenty-two-year-old mother when she said that it was God's mercy that saved her baby. While you fight the good fight of faith (i.e., trusting in God against all odds), the "Omnipotent God" will circumvent all prevailing, unprecedented circumstances and thereby make a way for you. God would make a way for your baby, even after several miscarriages have occurred, just as he made a way for baby Joassaint to remain alive and uninjured for seven days after a 7.0-magnitude earthquake with eight aftershocks on Tuesday, January 12, 2010, in Haiti.

Regardless of the mandrakes used, miscarriages continued robbing would-be mothers (at Jericho) of their unborn babies. What do you do when your mandrakes eventually work but you still don't get your baby because of miscarriages? The inhabitants of Jericho had a plan. They petitioned the Man of God—Elisha. Maybe God could do something! Maybe, if they depended completely on God for deliverance from miscarriages, He would remove the pollution and stop the miscarriages. Maybe if they fought the good fight of faith (1 Timothy 6:12, KJV) and called out to God, He would answer them and show them overwhelmingly marvelous things, the likes of which they have never seen (Jeremiah 33:3, KJV). Most assuredly, God did. Elisha obeyed God's instructions by taking salt from a new container and pouring it into the source of the underground water spring. The polluted waters were instantly purified. The ground was then saturated with clean water, and the miscarriages in man and beast stopped. If you had lived in Jericho at that time—mandrakes or no mandrakes—you would have had your baby after the purification of the polluted water. I'm sure that you're wondering what really happened that caused salt poured from a new container to instantly purify contaminated water. I had the same wondering experience until I realized a simple principle of life. Disobedience to God ultimately leads to death, but obedience to God leads to abundant life and prosperity. It was disobedience to God's express command not to rebuild Jericho (Joshua 6:26, KJV) that resulted in the encounter with an environmental catastrophe and miscarriages at Jericho. In contrast, it was obedience to God that stopped death and misery of life at Jericho (2 Kings 2:18–22, KJV).

Furthermore, it does not matter what caused the miscarriage. The persistent assurance of God's word will nullify and end any variant cause that is responsible for a miscarriage. Psalm 51:15 (KJV) entreats us, "And call upon me in the day of trouble: I will deliver thee, and thou shalt glorify me." When paraphrased, the text states that God invites us to call out to Him whenever we meet with any distress or adversity, and He will rescue us. Then we would praise and honor the Omnipotent God because our rescue and deliverance would be too uniquely phenomenal and beyond human. There are many mothers alive today, who have had lethal bouts with two or more miscarriages, and have lived on to conceive two or more babies. I have had the honor of meeting one such delightful mother, whom I would not name. She is now the thankful mother of three precious children after having endured at least two miscarriages.

Let us fast forward from that throwback experience at Jericho. Elisha has been dead longer than the establishment of any modern nation in the Western world. In many instances, the only mandrake we have left is time itself. Well, what if the mandrake of *time* is fast running out? What if that biological clock is close to its last *tick-tock*? Maybe the biological clock has already stopped. The hour hand, minute hand, and second hand have all stopped moving, and the pendulum is no longer swinging. When your only mandrake is time itself and time has run out, no more mandrakes remain. So, what does a man or woman do about preparation to conceive a baby when there are no mandrakes left? What do you do when it appears as if time itself has run out on you? Now that is a moment that can be described as a gonadotropic dysfunction compounded by an uncertain duration. That's a conundrum—a baby-making conundrum. That is exactly where Abraham and his wife Sarah found themselves when they started their preparation – in a baby-making conundrum.

CHAPTER 4

Menostop—Abraham and Sarah

TIME HAD RUN OUT for this older couple in the Bible. Abraham was now one hundred years old. His body had leaped into and was casually drifting in a new biological time-zone known as ARED (age-related erectile dysfunction) with andropause. Andropause is a condition associated with the decrease of the male hormone testosterone. Testosterone is a hormone produced by the human body. It is mainly produced in men by the testicles. Testosterone affects a man's appearance and sexual development. It stimulates sperm production as well as a man's sex drive. It also helps build muscle and bone mass. Testosterone production typically decreases with age. According to the American Urological

Association, about two out of ten men older than sixty years have low testosterone. That increases slightly to three out of ten men in their 70s and 80s. Abraham was one hundred years old.

Sarah was ninety years old, and her body was now so far past menopause that it had crossed over from post-menopause into *menostop*. If menostop sounds like a new word, it is. You have been first introduced to it here. At the current moment of my writing, there was no word in the English dictionary to appropriately describe the extreme extent of Sarah's improbable childbearing condition. As a result, I gave myself the latitude of coining a new word just for the purpose of making the point in this book. As the word menopause suggests, a pause is only a temporary halt in action. There is always the possibility of continuance regardless of the length of the pause. With Sarah, this was not a pause; it was over and done. Punto, final! Stop does not suggest any iota of continuance. Therefore, another word (with stop imbedded in it) was necessary and urgently needed. Out of this necessity appeared the term *menostop*. Necessity is truly the mother of invention. Here is how the Bible describes the biological condition of the respective bodies of Abraham and Sarah.

And being not weak in faith, he considered not his own body now dead, when he was about

an hundred years old, neither yet the deadness
of Sarah's womb (Romans 4:19, KJV)

Their respective biological baby-making apparatus was
literally dead. It was in that physical condition that God
informed this older couple that they were supposed to have
a baby.

> And God said unto Abraham, as for Sarai
> thy wife, thou shalt not call her name Sarai,
> but Sarah shall her name be. And I will bless
> her, and give thee a son also of her: yea, I
> will bless her, and she shall be a mother of
> nations; kings of people shall be of her. Then
> Abraham fell upon his face, and laughed, and
> said in his heart, Shall a child be born unto
> him that is an hundred years old? And shall
> Sarah, that is ninety years old, bear?" (Genesis
> 17:15–17, KJV)

If it were any human speaking, that would have been
adding insult to injury. However, the Omnipotent and
Sovereign Lord had spoken. With God all things are possible.
That is exactly what Abraham and Sarah believed, and they
acted on what they believed.

> He staggered not at the promise of God through
> unbelief; but was strong in faith, giving glory

to God; And being fully persuaded that, what he had promised, he was able also to perform. (Romans 4:20, KJV)

The uniqueness of this occurrence requires our utmost attention. As a result, let us peruse the situation and microscopically examine the action. A one-hundred-year-old man in Andropause with perennial age-related erectile dysfunction (ARED) and a ninety-year-old woman in menostop (way past post-menopause, i.e., the biological clock had stopped) agreed to make a baby together. Despite the obvious reality, Sarah had to begin believing that her reproductive life would jumpstart over the next three months, bring about ovulation, and culminate in conception for the first time in her ninety years of life. Abraham would also have had to believe ("beyond the shadow of a doubt") that his body would overwhelmingly increase testosterone productivity and radically realign his hormonal synchrony to produce healthy motile gametes (i.e., sperms). Then he must have trusted in the renewed coordination between visual stimulation, mental sexual arousal, and sustained blood profusion in the horizontal extension of his lower midsection. All that was necessary for copulation, which would trigger the launching of motile gametes on their journey of ascension to the Mount of Conception. This was not going to be a one-day demonstration or a same-day surgical operation. This was going to be a consistently repeated conjugal visitation over a three-month duration. Only after three months of obedience to this otherwise human impossibility would they expect to experience the conception of their baby. God's promise to Abraham specifically said that Sarah would give birth to a baby in exactly one year from the time that God spoke the promise.

But my covenant will I establish with Isaac, which Sarah shall bear unto thee at this set time in the next year. (Genesis 17:21, KJV)

Timing is of importance here. "In the next year" means in twelve months. Since it takes only nine months for a human baby to fully develop, that leaves three long months before Sarah would conceive. Three months of awakening to the reality of Sarah and Abraham's faith journey; three needed months to rediscover their emotional chemistry; three months to rekindle their physical activity; three crucial months before their date with destiny.

I imagine that Sarah and Abraham would have begun examining for signs of pregnancy sometime after the appointed date with destiny (i.e., nine months before the prophesied date of birth of their long-awaited baby). Meanwhile, they would have continued with conjugal activities, at least until Sarah was 100 percent sure she was pregnant. All of this—historical restoration of the human body, rekindling of conjugal activity, plunging deep into the uncharted waters of a faith journey—was started, empowered, sustained, and fulfilled by the Omnipotent God of Glory (in heaven). All this divine intervention was done because of the expectation of a baby.

Let me say it now. When mandrakes don't work, God works.

Nine months later, Abraham and Sarah would cuddle their new baby and name him Isaac (meaning "laughter"). They had laughed at God when He declared that they would have a baby long after their bodies had been reproductively waned: Genesis 17:17; 18:12 (KJV). After God had fulfilled His word to them, they were ready to laugh with God for the rest of their lives—by obeying God in naming the child Isaac Genesis 17:19; 21:3 (KJV). When mandrakes don't work, God works. Even if there are no mandrakes at all, God still works. When mandrakes don't work, Faith in God works.

Zero (0) Mandrakes + 2 Reproductively Dead Bodies = 1 Baby

God himself, without any mandrakes, rejuvenated Abraham's, and Sarah's sexual virility, installed brand-new reproductive fertility into their bodies, and blessed them with a miracle baby. Never again has such a biological feat been recorded in human history. Sarah lived another thirty-six years after the birth of Isaac, and although she did not have another child, she died at the precious age of one hundred and twenty-seven in perfect virile condition. God never mentioned that her newfound condition had waned - Genesis 23:1 (KJV). Oh! I feel a divine commercial in my cranium: When the doctors say they can't do anything about it, God will fix it. When God fixes it, He maintains it. It might have been a while since you have functioned, but God can handle it. He will salvage it, dust it off (i.e., "get rid of the cobwebs"), revive it, and keep it, just like it was when you first discovered it.

Just remember that God designed it. He installed it and maintained it. That is why only God and God alone can engineer it. Just like seed germination, only God can determine conception. As for Abraham, his rejuvenated sexual virility and newly installed fertility lasted for at least another half century (fifty years). After Sarah died, Abraham took a second wife, Keturah, and had six more sons. For Abraham, God had fixed it (i.e., He had restored it) and kept it, and when Abraham died at the ripe old age of 175, he still had it. Genesis 25:1–7 (KJV). Furthermore, Ecclesiastes 3:14 (KJV) categorically says,

> I know that, whatsoever God doeth, it shall
> be forever: nothing can be put to it, nor any
> thing taken from it: and God doeth it, that
> men should fear before Him.

If you have ever had relatives, friends, loved ones, parents, or in-laws who constantly ask, "When are you going to give me a grandchild (or a pretty niece or handsome nephew)," you would know that it can be somewhat overbearing. Sometimes, it is downright frustrating. Please listen, everybody. We cannot give ourselves a baby, because it is not in anyone's power to give herself or himself a baby. Yet, those whom you expect to be more sensitive to your situation continue asking—what has become—that Irritating Question. They ask it as if they had given you something to keep and you have been taking too long to return it. So, they need to give you a scolding reminder to receive it. Well, if that is frustrating and irritating, imagine being reminded daily about it, from morning till evening.

It might cause you to lift your hands into the air and your head to the Heavens and desperately ask, "God, please remember me."

CHAPTER 5

God Remembered Her—Hannah

IF YOU WOULD describe the rivalry between Leah and Rachel as intense and unbecoming, then the tension between Peninnah and Hannah was toxic and repulsive. When compared to the social atmosphere between Leah and Rachel, this was déjà vu, compounded by mirages and hallucinations, yet real and substantive. If the earlier sentence gave you mental swirls as though you had been physically spinning around, then this is just a taste of the mental and psychological swirling that Hannah was subjected to every year on their annual family trip. Oh, by the way, that annual family trip was in fact a worship pilgrimage.

"Worship who?" you might ask. Just try not to become all sanctimonious and self-righteous now. Similar scenarios like that are enacted weekly at many Sunday worship services and Sabbath worship services. Peninnah insulted, ridiculed, and harassed Hannah because of her inability to conceive a child.

> Now there was a certain man ... of mount Ephraim, and his name was Elkanah. ... And he had two wives; the name of the one was Hannah, and the name of the other Peninnah: and Peninnah had children, but Hannah had no children. And this man went up out of his city yearly to worship and to sacrifice unto the Lord of hosts in Shiloh. ...And when the time was that Elkanah offered, he gave to Peninnah his wife, and to all her sons and her daughters, portions: But unto Hannah he gave a worthy part; for he loved Hannah: but the Lord had shut up her womb. And her adversary also provoked her sore, for to make her fret, because the Lord had shut up her womb. And as he did so year by year, when she went up to the house of the Lord, so she provoked her; therefore she wept, and did not eat. (1 Samuel 1:1–7, KJV)

It's bad enough to mock somebody about a defect or condition over which they have no control. However, hurling verbal insults and constant public harassment over a woman's inability to have a baby is taking disregard to another level—a deplorable and unparalleled level. Open insult with ridicule and constant harassment was Peninnah's annual gourmet three-course meal, verbally served to Hannah. Every year, after presenting their offering of thanks, it was customary that the entire family (Elkanah, both wives, and all the children) would unite in a solemn and joyous feast. During these festivities, Elkanah would give gifts to Peninnah and each of her children (boys and girls). However, twice as many gifts were given to Hannah even though she had no child. This was Elkanah's way of showing his affection for Hannah just as if she had borne him children.

Well, Elkanah's public display of affection towards Hannah incited Peninnah's anger. She would become enraged with a torrent of jealousy and unleash an avalanche of taunting words on Hannah. Although Peninnah was the second wife, she claimed precedence over Hannah. Peninnah perceived that because she had given her husband children, she was more favored of God than Hannah. Peninnah even put forward the idea that the reason Hannah couldn't have a baby was that God was not pleased with her. In other words, Peninnah suggested that Hannah was under a curse from God as if that were true. At this stage, Hannah had had enough of this demeaning treatment. She could no longer endure that torture. She looked for help. Although she lived in the same geographic area as Leah and Rachel, where literal mandrakes still grow until our current time, she did not turn to mandrakes for help. She neither opted for any literal or figurative mandrakes. She unburdened her grief-stricken mind with unrestrained lament to God—Jehovah Jireh—her provider.

There are moments in life when we come face-to-face with dire circumstances and we instinctively turn our hearts to heaven and exclaim, "God, do something!" In those peculiar life-threatening situations, we turn to a Divine Power outside of ourselves and cry out in desperation, "God! Help me." You do not remember any mandrakes, best friends, husbands, wives, sisters, brothers, fathers, mothers, or any significant others. You somehow don't call on humanity. You reach out for divinity. Hannah called on God Almighty, who is from Eternity to Eternity.

> And she was in bitterness of soul, and prayed
> unto the Lord, and wept sore. And she vowed
> a vow, and said, O Lord of hosts, if thou
> wilt indeed look on the affliction of thine
> handmaid, and remember me, and not forget
> thine handmaid, but wilt give unto thine
> handmaid a man child, then I will give him
> unto the Lord all the days of his life, and there

shall no razor come upon his head. (1 Samuel 1:10–11, KJV)

Occasionally, your intensity of purpose can be completely misunderstood and misinterpreted. Moving lips while in a prayer posture but no words being uttered? Eli observed a little longer. Again, with optical detail, he saw her moving mandible but heard nothing audible. He quickly formed his opinion and later made an improper declaration.

And it came to pass, as she continued praying before the Lord, that Eli marked her mouth. Now Hannah, she spake in her heart; only her lips moved, but her voice was not heard: therefore Eli thought she had been drunken. (1 Samuel 1:12–13, KJV)

What follows next are words from Eli's public declaration based on a misguided opinion followed by an ensuing close encounter with Hannah.

And Eli said unto her, How long wilt thou be drunken? Put away thy wine from thee. And Hannah answered and said, No, my Lord, I am a woman of a sorrowful spirit: I have drunk neither wine nor strong drink, but have poured out my soul before the Lord. Count not thine handmaid for a daughter of Belial:

> for out of the abundance of my complaint
> and grief have I spoken hitherto. Then Eli
> answered and said, Go in peace: and the God
> of Israel grant thee thy petition that thou hast
> asked of him. (1 Samuel 1:14–17, KJV)

What a turnaround? Eli shifted from making a formal accusation to making a prophetic announcement. In that very moment also, Hannah learned that she would have a baby. Then her emotions experienced a seismic shift from discouragement to encouragement. Hannah was no longer sad but glad.

> And she said, Let thine handmaid find grace
> in thy sight. So the woman went her way, and
> did eat, and her countenance was no more sad.
> (1 Samuel 1:18, KJV)

She went to worship one way and left another way. Whenever we go to God, we should always leave a different person compared to when we entered His presence. Bartimaeus went to Jesus as a blind man. When he left, he was a seeing man. Nicodemus went to Jesus as a ruler of the Jews. When he left Jesus, he was a subject of the King of the Jews. The paralytic was taken by friends to Jesus through the roof as a lame and sinful man. When he left Jesus, he walked through the door as a healed and forgiven man. Hannah went to worship God at Shiloh with the uncertainty of a baby. She left God's House at Shiloh with the assurance of a baby.

> Then Eli answered and said, Go in peace: and the God of Israel grant thee thy petition that thou hast asked of him. (1 Samuel 1:17, KJV)

However, God's assurance required the accompaniment of human performance. So, after a 14-mile journey and about six to eight hours later, when they were back home, they did not waste any time. Now armed with a promise and a renewed purpose, Elkanah and Hannah went to work on that baby.

> And they rose up in the morning early, and worshipped before the Lord, and returned, and came to their house to Ramah: and Elkanah knew Hannah his wife; and the Lord remembered her. (1 Samuel 1:19, KJV)

Less than one week after returning home to Ramah, Hannah became pregnant. Now allow me to explain how I arrived at that conclusion. The above inserted text of 1 Samuel 1:19 (KJV) states that after they returned home, Elkanah knew his wife Hannah. The term "knew his wife" simply means that they had coital sexual activity. The return trip home lasted less than a day (six to eight hours). Even if they took one or two days to recuperate from the exhausting cross-country travel, there would still be five more days to complete a week. Now the very same Bible text, in 1 Samuel 1:19 (KJV), also says that when they engaged in "Baby-making activity" that "the Lord remembered her" (i.e., remembered Hannah). Deductive reasoning would lead one to conclude that the term "the Lord remembered her" is another way of saying that God caused her to conceive. Therefore, the immediate logical conclusion would be that Hannah became pregnant a few days after returning home. Nevertheless, I solemnly owe you an explanation about that term, "the Lord remembered her." Way back in chapter 1, I promised you that I would explain what that really means. Permit me the honor of fulfilling that promise now.

After many years of being unable to conceive, it was said about Rachel, "And God remembered Rachel, and God hearkened to her, and opened her womb" (Genesis 30:22, KJV). In the current chapter of this book, similar words are also used to describe Hanna's new condition after many years of being unable to conceive a baby.

> And Elkanah knew Hannah his wife; and the
> Lord remembered her. 1 Samuel 1:19 (KJV)

The word *zakar* (pronounced zaw-kar) is the original Hebrew word from which the English word "remembered" was translated on both occasions. In Genesis 30:22 (KJV) *zakar* is translated as "remembered," and in 1 Samuel 1:19

(KJV), it literally means "to mark for the purpose of being recognized."

God caused both Rachel and Hannah to each conceive a special boy child so that the life and significance of each child would cause each woman to be rightfully acknowledged as "special mothers" as compared with just being "the other woman." Moreover, because of the life and existence of both boys (Joseph and Samuel), their respective mothers would become elevated from obscurity in the family to prominence in the Hebrew nation. Both mothers would later be established into the Mothers Hall of Fame of Planet Earth.

Let me explain. By naming her son Samuel, Hannah was forever publishing to the universe that God—not the doctor, not any form of mandrake—had given her a baby. The Hebrew name Samuel, translated into English, could mean "God has heard" or "name of God." It is more likely that Hannah intended the first (i.e., "God has heard"). Therefore, just by calling the name Samuel, the world is forever proclaiming to the truth that God heard Hannah's prayer. In other words, every time the child would have been seen in the village, the neighborhood, or the Temple, people would have to say, "That is God's answer to Hannah's prayer." That is evidence that God heard Hannah's prayer. The mere existence of the child testifies aloud that God heard Hanna's prayer.

Furthermore, Samuel was dedicated for God's holy service by Hannah and left at the Temple in the care of Eli, the Temple high priest. This dedication led to the child Samuel becoming Israel's judge, teacher, and prophet. Samuel became the chief ruler in the nation of Israel. He pioneered the restoration of his people to walking again in obedience to God, by travelling throughout the nation and teaching the Law of God. Then he set up formal schools of learning, where God's Law was taught. These were called Schools of the Prophets. Wherever Samuel went, people would react like observers in the Allstate Insurance television commercial. During that commercial, people in the restaurant identified the pitchman verbally by repeating the mantra, "Safe drivers save 40 percent." If it were Samuel that had walked into the leading burger restaurant, people would have been saying, "That's God *has heard* Hanna's prayer!" Yes, "God *has heard* Hanna's prayer." That's him right there! That's totally him!"

After leaving Samuel at the Temple to grow up in the care of Eli, the high priest, Hannah gave birth to five more children, three more sons and two daughters.

> Moreover, his mother made him a little coat, and brought it to him from year to year, when she came up with her husband to offer the yearly sacrifice. And Eli blessed Elkanah and his wife, and said, The Lord give thee seed of this woman for the loan which is lent to the Lord. And they went unto their own home. And the Lord visited Hannah, so that

she conceived, and bare three sons and two daughters. And the child Samuel grew before the Lord. (1 Samuel 2:19–21, KJV)

Let us not forget Rachel. God also remembered her (*zakar*). God marked Rachel so that she also would be forever recognized, by granting her a special boy child whom she named Joseph.

And God remembered Rachel, and God hearkened to her, and opened her womb. And she conceived, and bare a son; and said, God hath taken away my reproach: And she called his name Joseph; and said, The Lord shall add to me another son. (Genesis 30:22–24, KJV)

The Hebrew word from which 'Joseph' was translated is the word Yoseph and literally means "may He add." Yoseph is derived from the root word Yasaph, which literally means "to add." Rachel named her boy child, Joseph, in anticipation that God would add another son to her first child. So, God granted Rachel another son.

And they journeyed from Bethel; and there was but a little way to come to Ephrata: and Rachel travailed, and she had hard labour. And it came to pass, when she was in hard labour, that the midwife said unto her, Fear

not; thou shalt have this son also. And it came
to pass, as her soul was in departing, (for she
died) that she called his name Benoni: but his
father called him Benjamin. And Rachel died,
and was buried in the way to Ephrata, which
is Bethlehem. (Genesis 35:16–19, KJV)

This inspired pronouncement, in the name Joseph ("may
He add") for her personal application would also prove to be
prophetic in the development of Israel as a nation. As a result
of Joseph being sold into Egypt and a predicted international
famine, the whole household of Jacob went to live in Egypt.
They went into Egypt totaling seventy in number (Genesis
46:27, KJV) and multiplied into a great nation. Religious
Historians estimate that they were 2 to 3 million at the time
of the Exodus under Moses: from a mere seventy multiplying
into three million. Who did God use to start this exponential
population growth of a nation within a nation? Rachel's
boy child Joseph ("may He add"). God had added because
of Joseph.

Joseph, may God add, would also feature in the addition
and accumulation of food in Egypt in preparation for a
famine of international proportion.

And Joseph was thirty years old when he
stood before Pharaoh king of Egypt. And
Joseph went out from the presence of Pharaoh

and went throughout all the land of Egypt. And in the seven plenteous years the earth brought forth by handfuls. And he gathered up all the food of the seven years, which were in the land of Egypt, and laid up the food in the cities: the food of the field, which was round about every city, laid he up in the same. And Joseph gathered corn as the sand of the sea, very much, until he left numbering; for it was without number. … And the famine was over all the face of the earth: and Joseph opened all the storehouses, and sold unto the Egyptians; and the famine waxed sore in the land of Egypt. And all countries came into Egypt to Joseph for to buy corn; because that the famine was so sore in all lands. (Genesis 41:46–49; 56–57, KJV)

Because of Rachel's boy child (Joseph), God had added enough food in the barns and warehouses of Egypt to supply an international market during the seven years of a world famine. Joseph lived to the perfect Egyptian age of 110 and died. Now, hundreds of years after both Rachel and Joseph had died, God was still adding hope to the Hebrew nation's posterity through Joseph's dead body. Before Joseph died, he and his relatives agreed to a solemn oath, that they would not leave his embalmed body in Egypt when they would have been delivered from bondage in Egypt.

> And Joseph said unto his brethren, I die: and God will surely visit you, and bring you out of this land unto the land which he sware to Abraham, to Isaac, and to Jacob. And Joseph took an oath of the children of Israel, saying, God will surely visit you, and ye shall carry up my bones from hence. So Joseph died, being an hundred and ten years old: and they embalmed him, and he was put in a coffin in Egypt. (Genesis 50:24–26, KJV)

At that time, the Hebrews were a free people in Egypt. That was at least two hundred years before Moses was born and more than three hundred years before the Exodus. Will you please count with me? Joseph was thirty years old at the time that he interpreted Pharaoh's dream about the seven years of prosperity (plenty), followed by seven years of economic depression (famine).

> And Joseph was thirty years old when he stood before Pharaoh king of Egypt. And Joseph went out from the presence of Pharaoh, and went throughout all the land of Egypt. And in the seven plenteous years the earth brought forth by handfuls. (Genesis 41:46–47, KJV)

After the seven years of prosperity and seven years of famine, he would have been fourteen years older (30 + 14 = 44). Joseph would have been forty-four years old at the end of the famine. However, Joseph's father (Jacob) and his relatives went up to Egypt the year before the famine ended. Therefore, Joseph was forty-three years old when his father, Jacob, and Joseph's relatives entered Egypt. Since Joseph died at the age of 110 (Genesis 24:26, KJV), he would have spent the last sixty-seven years of his life with his relatives in Egypt.

110 (Joseph's age at death) - 43 (his age when relatives went to Egypt) = 67 years

Therefore, at the death of Joseph, the Hebrews (of Israel) had been in Egypt for only sixty-seven years. However, Israel would spend 430 years in Egypt:

> Now the sojourning of the children of Israel, who dwelt in Egypt, was four hundred and thirty years. And it came to pass at the end of the four hundred and thirty years, even the selfsame day it came to pass, that all the hosts of the Lord went out from the land of Egypt. (Exodus 12:40–41, KJV)

Hence, there would be yet another 363 years before the Exodus of Israel under Moses:

430 years (Israel's time in Egypt) – 67 years
(time spent at Joseph's death) = 363 years

Thus, the presence of Joseph's embalmed body added encouragement to his people (the Hebrews) during times of discouragement, totaling more than 350 years. It was a physical reminder that God would one day deliver the Hebrews from their hardships and the burden of slavery under Pharaoh in Egypt.

And Joseph took an oath of the children of Israel, saying, God will surely visit you, and ye shall carry up my bones from hence. (Genesis 50:52, KJV)

When Rachel's baby was born, God had added so much joy to her life that she named him Joseph ("may He add") or ("may God add"). Just before Rachel's death, God had added another son (Benjamin) to her life just as Joseph's name proclaimed. When Joseph was bought by Ishmaelites and taken to Egypt, where he was resold as a slave to Potiphar, God was adding the forerunner of a deliverer (Moses) for Israel. When Joseph—Rachel's special boy child—died, God was adding hope for Israel before their harassment during slavery in Egypt. After more than four hundred years, God was still adding because of Rachel's baby boy. Rachel, who had been dead for almost 450 years, was still being recognized when Joseph's bones were taken out of Egypt by Moses during the Exodus and later buried in Canaan after Joshua led Israel across the Jordan River.

And Moses took the bones of Joseph with him: for he had straitly sworn the children of Israel, saying, God will surely visit you; and ye shall carry up my bones away hence with you. (Exodus 13:19, KJV) - And the bones of Joseph, which the children of Israel brought up out of Egypt, buried they in Shechem, in a parcel of ground which Jacob bought of the sons of Hamor the father of Shechem for an hundred pieces of silver: and it became the inheritance of the children of Joseph. (Joshua 24:32, KJV)

God had added Joseph, in advance, to Egypt to make a way as a forerunner for Israel. Now, God was adding Joseph's embalmed body to a resting place beside his father, Jacob, in Canaan. Whatever God had added through Joseph was proclaimed and prophesied by his mother Rachel just by naming him Joseph ("may he add" or "may God add").

Without any mandrakes, God had *heard* (Samuel). Without any mandrakes, God had *added* (Joseph). So, be encouraged. If you're like Hannah and can't bear this torture of being childless any longer, if you've heard enough of that Irritating Question (i.e., "When are you going to have a baby?), if time is no longer on your side or you're on the other side of time, just remember this simple fact: *When your mandrakes don't work, God works.* When, like Hannah and

Rachel, you call out to God in earnestness, God will answer you and show you great and mighty things about which your mind have not even conceived (Jeremiah 33:3, KJV). God will *zakar* you—He will *remember* you. God will mark you with a special boy child so that because of the child, you will be forever recognized as a mother, his mother. You might be thinking that you are not Sarah and Abraham, nor Rachel or Hannah. That happened for them because of who they were, Bible greats. I am not them, so that does not apply to me. If you are still reading and that is where your thoughts are, I had similar thoughts before it happened to me.

CHAPTER 6

Then It Happened to Me

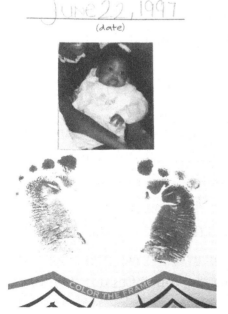

WE WERE MARRIED for six years but had no children—partly due to circumstances beyond our control and partly by our choice. Like many internationally married couples, we lived in different countries for the first few years of marriage. I can hear you thinking, so let me prevent your mind from wandering. You might drift into vain imaginings. Conjugal visitations and delayed gratification were part of our common mode of operation. In addition, there was constant dependence on divine strength to resist temptation, coupled with a conscious decision to be true to God and faithful to each other. God once kept a heathen king from sexual sin without that king ever asking to be kept from sinning:

> And God said unto him in a dream, Yea,
> I know that thou didst this in the integrity
> of thy heart; for I also withheld thee from
> sinning against me: therefore suffered I thee
> not to touch her. (Genesis 20:6, KJV)

That being true, how much more would the same God do for his children who are asking and pleading to him? Psalm 121:5 (KJV) had informed me that the Lord is my keeper and in my simple mind, I thought it was supporting and reinforcing Genesis 20:6 (KJV). So I reasoned that God would keep me from sinning generally and from sexual sin. If you are inclined to think, as many of us do, "Oh, that's hard." I hear you. I also hear God saying that He is "able to do exceeding, abundantly above all that we ask or think" (Ephesians 3:20, KJV). Then, what I read in Jude became the clincher for me, bolstering my confidence in God's keeping power: "Now unto him that is able to keep you from falling, and to present you faultless before the presence of his glory with exceeding joy." (Jude 1:24, KJV)

Then I thought, *did you hear that? It says that He said that He's able to keep you from falling and present you faultless.* Immediately, a calm assurance enveloped me, and I knew that if God kept Abimelech, king of Gerar, in Genesis 20 (KJV), from sinning sexually, He would keep me. He would also keep my young wife. In fact, He has kept us for the past thirty-five years, and there is no chance of Him losing His keeping power. In that moment, Philippians 4:13 (KJV) came alive for me: "I can do all things through Christ who strengthens me."

So, there we were: six years after the wedding and no children. For three years we had heard that inquiring question about a baby. I heard it from friends, relatives, the church community, and neighbors living on our street. At one point, it looked as though I was hearing it from anybody, just any random somebody. While we were out shopping or just casually sightseeing, observant, mannerly, well-meaning creatures of God (*Homo sapiens* of our kind) would just look at us and say, "You two are married, right? I hope you don't mind me asking. I was observing you from over there, and from the look of things, I knew you must be married. Congratulations."

Those encounters, though unexpected, would be good up until that point. Then the question would be asked. Whatever the reason, they just had to ask that question. "Any little ones yet? You look like you would be great parents." Then the encounter would be over. Those were *Close Encounters of the Baby-Questioning Kind.* As those occurrences became more frequent, the impact of the question began to stir up emotions of irritation. Soon, that simple, well-meaning question became the Irritating Question. The people were not intentional irritants. It was our inability to supply an expected answer that irritated us. Various mandrakes, including two rounds of in vitro fertilization, and still no conception. The casual observer had no idea what we were experiencing. When the doctor cautiously expressed little hope of anything happening, we turned our full attention to seeking divine intervention. Like many people, we compared ourselves to Abraham and Sarah, Jacob and Rachel, Elkanah and Hannah, Mr. and Mrs. Manoah—Sampson's parents in Judges 13 (KJV)—and Zacharias and Elizabeth, the aged parents of John the Baptist in Luke 1 (KJV). Can you see where this was going? There was absolutely no way you could ever see yourself measuring up to those people. Those were the great ones. That is why they are in the Bible (that was our reasoning in that moment). You only read about them; you don't become them. So, I began talking to myself again. "No! No! No! I'm not going out like that. I can't give up." After all, the Lord had assured me of being a family man many years before, or I would have remained a eunuch for the Gospel's sake. That is why I trusted the Lord to find me a wife, and now that we had been married, there should have been children—at least *one* child, just *one*.

Therefore, there had to be something in the Bible for people like me. In times of distress, trouble, confusion, perplexity, or any kind of difficulty, we had been encouraged to read the Psalms. So, I began reading the Psalms. Reading became searching. Searching became microscopic scrutinizing. I didn't want to miss anything. Maybe the Lord would show me something, something that would satisfy my longing, something that would quench my thirst. There was nowhere else to turn, so I was digging in and concentrating. I keenly examined every minute detail. Then I got over to Psalm 113 (KJV). It's a short psalm. It looked familiar to me. The first three verses had become frequently used phrases in public worship sessions and corporate prayers, especially verse three.

> Praise ye the Lord. Praise, O ye servants of the Lord, praise the name of the Lord. Blessed be the name of the Lord from this time forth and for evermore. From the rising of the sun unto

the going down of the same the Lord's name

is to be praised. (Psalm 113:1–3, KJV)

Nevertheless, I needed to concentrate on every verse with meticulous scrutiny and examine every word with microscopic intensity. Most certainly, I couldn't afford to miss anything that was in it for me. Then down in the very last verse, I saw something that jumped out at me. The words jumped up right off the page to start a fire inside me. That was Serendipity.

He maketh the barren woman to keep house,

and to be a joyful mother of children. Praise

ye the Lord. (Psalm 113:9, KJV)

That statement there in Psalm 113:9 (KJV) is for anybody. That was written there and waiting all the while just for me. That wasn't about Zacharias and Elizabeth, nor Jacob and Rachel. It wasn't for Abraham and Sarah, Elkanah and Hannah, nor Mr. and Mrs. Manoah. Oh, Serendipity, Serendipity! I am glad I found something by accident, and it was waiting there just for me. It had been written just for me!

After a moment of jubilation, I hurried over to show my wife what I had discovered. Then it became shared treasure. It had then become what *we* had discovered. That day in October 1994, we applied that promise to our situation and trusted that the benefits of this promise would be fulfilled in us. Then my wife's emotions started to experience a seismic shift, just like Hannah's. They shifted from discouragement to encouragement, from sad to glad, from pessimistic to optimistic. *God's assurances to man always require corresponding action, for us to experience the fulfillment.* Sometimes that action is performed by God alone. On other occasions, our exact and total obedience is required in cooperation with God's omnipotence. Therefore, it was time for preparation. I am not talking about the physical preparation per se. That was a given. The more needed preparation was in making accommodation for the yet unfulfilled expectation—a baby. Recognizing the Psalm 113:9 (KJV) promise alone was, to our minds, like New Year's fireworks invading the darkness of a midnight sky with a kaleidoscope of glory. We began to see things differently, and we were motivated to act accordingly. It had not even been the beginning of her first trimester, and my wife had already begun acting like a mother. The mental stimulation of Psalm 113:9 (KJV) promoted some unforeseen action.

In early December 1994, my not-yet Pregnant Wife raised an open objection during the process of our local church elections. As was customary, in the privacy of the nominating committee, she showed her objection. She calmly stated her opinion, then waited for any reaction.

"I am objecting to my husband being elected to any position." When questioned about the rationale behind her expressed opinion, she said it was due to her and her husband's ongoing family situation. After my wife had gracefully departed from the presence of the stunned committee, her expressed opinion was enough for the nominating committee to reevaluate and withdraw my name from that single elected position. It was the most awkward experience for me because all this was happening right before my eyes since I was the chairperson of that committee. I could not risk explaining anything to the committee without raising domestic questions about our marriage harmony, so I kept quiet. Silence is golden when you don't have the right answer to give. Then I began to internally question myself, whether this was some form of spiritual interference and that my wife had become an innocent victim of the adversary. We drove home from church in silence, except for when I broke the monotony by casually requesting to share something with my wife when we would have arrived at our destination. During the silence, I was reminded (by an unseen visitor) that I had agreed with my wife to put our faith into action by making physical preparation for the answer to our prayer for a baby while there was yet no pregnancy. Then I questioned myself. Is that what this objection to my election might have been? The answer became an unspoken rebuke for me. My wife had taken a leap of faith in ensuring that her husband would be free from external duties during her first pregnancy. As a result, his attention to her care would not be redirected elsewhere nor distracted. Contrarily, I had unreasonably began questioning her spiritual stability. That silent rebuke was enough for me. I almost broke down in tears, but I was still driving, so I managed to maintain enough emotional stability to get us home safely. We arrived home incident-free. When my wife reminded me that I had requested to share something with her when we had arrived home, I humbly declined. God had scolded me into submission. That moment would mark the beginning of my undivided attention to my wife. Although she might have been unaware of it, I had begun my holistic critical observation.

In January 1995, my wife announced to me that she had an early Valentine's Day gift for me. That should have been an obvious signal for me. Who shows a Valentine's Day gift before that special day? Then I became eager to hear and more uncomfortable while waiting to hear. When cautiously urged, my wife lovingly disclosed that she had recently discovered that she was pregnant – *Boom-shaka-laka! Boom-shaka-laka!*

That was way better than any open-floor basketball dunk. The sweet sound of the word *pregnant* had "Taken Me Higher," higher than Ike and Tina Turner's *"Boom-shaka-laka, boom-shaka-laka"*. We had just been taken higher: from just husband and wife to expecting parents, from an ordinary woman to the esteemed category of mother; from the lowly status of man to the privileged company of fatherhood.

There was one caveat to our blessing. My wife wanted to keep it a secret until the end of the first trimester. She was not ready for anyone to know about our pregnancy. It could have been the presumed fear of "Let's wait until we know everything will be okay." Of course, I agreed. To tell you the truth, I felt so blessed at God answering our prayers that I would have agreed to anything my wife wanted at that point. Nevertheless, man has his ways, and God has his.

> For my thoughts are not your thoughts, neither are your ways my ways, saith the Lord.
> (Isaiah 55:8, KJV)

There was a newcomer to our church. My wife had asked me to befriend this newcomer during a tent revival my church had conducted. When the young lady came to the church, she was pregnant. My wife loves to minister to new believers, so she told me to go and have a conversation with the young lady. My wife was still ushering at the time and could not go and sit with the newcomer right away. I did exactly as my wife asked. As a result, my wife was able to minister to the newcomer after she gave birth to her baby, especially because that baby was very ill and remained in the hospital after the mother's discharge. The newcomer's baby was eventually sent home, and my wife went over to the newcomer's home and gave her a stuffed animal for the baby. Little by little the newcomer was engrafted into our family.

During the process of not knowing which way God would lead, as I mentioned earlier, we tried the mandrake of in vitro fertilization. My wife and I went to an appointment, during which the doctor said something was wrong with one of her fallopian tubes. She was so upset. I didn't know what to do, so I took her over to our friend's (the newcomer) house. Our friend was more like a sister. Her name is Madeia. She took my wife upstairs and consoled her, prayed with her, and gave her gifts to make her feel better. It was some months after that sisterly encounter with Madeia that my wife became pregnant.

Now while my wife and I vowed not to reveal the pregnancy for the first three months, God had another plan. One day our sister, Madeia, called and asked to speak with me. My wife informed her that I was at a church meeting and wouldn't be home for hours. Madeia asked my wife if it was okay for her to tell my wife about the dream she had. My wife said it was fine. Madeia was afraid to tell her, but she felt compelled to share since I was not around. Madeia told my wife that she had a dream that my wife was three months pregnant and concealing the pregnancy. Can you imagine the mixed emotions of shock and jubilation that seized me when I later learned about their conversation? *Learning about my wife's pregnancy through a dream was a revelation for Madeia. Her revelation became my confirmation that this was God's doing.*

My wife responded to Madeia by saying, "Okay, I will tell Malcolm you called." Consequently, my wife and I decided we would reveal the prized good news during the next Sabbath. After sunset that next Friday, we made a three-way conference call to Madeia.

I said to Madeia, "I know it has been a week since you spoke with my wife, but my wife and I wanted to return your call together." Then I said, "The dream you had is true. My wife is pregnant." We rejoiced all over again. We were on a *new high*. Once again, we were taken higher: from husband and wife to expecting parents, from an ordinary woman to the esteemed category of mother; from the lowly status of man to the privileged state of fatherhood. We reminisced about that life-changing moment. Suddenly, we had become ready to answer the formerly dreaded question. In fact, we now looked forward to being asked The Question. Its effect would no longer produce irritation. In fact, The Question would now promptly produce an instant thrill of jubilation followed by an aftermath of satisfaction. Psalm 113:9 (KJV) had done what mandrakes (pregnancy-enhancing methods) could not do. Oh, when mandrakes don't work, God works. He works through His spoken word. In the beginning, "He spake and it was done. He commanded and it stood fast" (Psalm 33:9, KJV).

Have you ever considered what would have happened in the beginning if God's spoken word had no authority nor ability to do something? Let me indulge your imagination. When God said, "Let there be light," the world would have remained in darkness, and we would not be here if there was no power in the Word of God. In fact, God assures us that whatever He says comes to pass.

So shall my word be that goeth forth out of
my mouth: it shall not return unto me void,
but it shall accomplish that which I please, and
it shall prosper in the thing whereto I sent it.
(Isaiah 55:11, KJV)

Furthermore, God has revealed to us that He holds his
word in higher esteem than his very name.

I will worship toward thy holy temple ... for
thou hast magnified thy word above all thy
name. (Psalm 138:2, KJV)

In the moment of our greatest need, God's word in Psalm
113:9 (KJV) accomplished what pleased Him and prospered
in my wife's pregnancy and the birth of a full-term boy baby.
So, finally, it had happened for us. It had happened for my
wife. As a result, I could safely say, it had happened to *me*.
God's word had become a living reality for us, and that was
only the melting of a great iceberg at the foot of a glacier.
The slow-moving glacier of childlessness had begun to melt
rapidly and career down the steep slope of infertility. It left
behind a straightened river valley flowing with the warm
waters of fertility.

After Rachel named her first son Joseph ("may He add,"
"may God add"), God added another son to her, Benjamin.
After Hannah named her first son Samuel ("God has heard"),
the reproductive echo of those words kept rebounding from

her womb for five more children. In like manner, after my wife conceived and gave birth to our son, God blessed us with a daughter. Hallelujah! Hallelujah! Hallelujah! However, sometime after the birth of our son we had become so caught up in the rapture of parenting that we had forgotten what Psalm 113:9 (KJV) said. We had faithfully claimed every word of that promise and God would make good exactly what he had promised:

> God is not a man, that he should lie, nor a son of man, that He should repent. Has He said, and will He not do it? Or has He spoken and will He not make it good *and* fulfill it? (Numbers 23:19, Amplified Bible)

Just before our son's first birthday, my wife conceived a second time. That was precisely the day that I was informed about what I had done. Temporarily, I had gotten into trouble with the Pregnancy Police. My wife had become pregnant unexpectedly, and I was the responsible party. The first time, she praised God for causing her to become pregnant. However, this time, she blamed me. I was left standing there dumbfounded. Our son was walking and talking, and we had been enjoying every moment of his presence. Nevertheless, the child was growing, monetary expenses were quickly increasing, and our financial resources seemed to be depleting. As first-time parents, we had felt as if we were just managing. Those are conditions under which any mother might discover she was pregnant again and not welcome such news. Therefore, I got into trouble. In my defense, I didn't write Psalm 113:9 (KJV)! So before holding anyone responsible for my wife's second pregnancy, we needed to reexamine Psalm 113:9 (KJV) with more scrutiny. I ran to the Bible and found Psalm 113:9 (KJV) easily because we had bookmarked it. Three words attracted me: "mother of children," especially the word "children." My situation was instantly transformed. There it was. God, not me, had promised to make her a *mother of children*. I hastened back to my wife with the open Bible. My countenance had changed from worry to glee. My wife looked puzzlingly at me. As I showed her the word "children" in Psalm 113:9 (KJV), she smiled happily, thanked God spontaneously, and praised Him profusely. God was once again responsible for my wife's pregnancy. Hallelujah to the King of Glory! I could then live happily ever after with an unspoken and dignified plea of "Not Guilty."

CHAPTER 7

Mandrakes or No Mandrakes?
(Just Venting)

LET US TAKE a few moments to acknowledge the unfortunate reality of being temporarily unable to conceive a baby. Let us acknowledge the ongoing reality of childlessness that severely affects numerous families. It was once our reality (i.e., my wife and I), and it is still the current and ongoing reality of thousands of people. The unfortunate reality of not being able to personally experience the blessing of conception has spawned a cacophony of emotions in most of us. Sometimes, it feels like the prolonged imprisonment of a stifling agony, from which you are yearning to be set free. While in that cell block of the solitary confinement of temporary barrenness, you begin to ask yourself, "Is there anybody out there who has the key? Is there anything that can provide a remedy?" For some people, mandrakes have been the remedy. As for me, I have discovered that only God in heaven has the key. So, when mandrakes did not work for me, God's handiwork came through for me. Therefore, it is my personal conclusion that, when mandrakes do not work, God works. So, take it from me: when there is no other remedy for your apparent infertility or conception inability, Jehovah Jireh—the Almighty God—has the key. He is the solution to all facets of your agonies. If you can partner with Him, He will remove the cause of your current agony and release you from your circumstantial cell block of temporary infertility.

Considering all things, one could not adequately discuss the topic of childbirth without confronting labor pains. In like manner, it would be remiss to discuss temporary infertility without addressing the pain endured by thousands of people longing for their conception of a baby. Now, while labor pains are the direct result of the actual process of birth, the pain of temporary infertility is not merely the result of the various unsuccessful attempts at becoming pregnant. That pain is mainly inflicted on would-be parents through some uniquely strange and extraordinary verbal comments, unusual requests, bold-faced questions, presumptuous demands, and downright coldhearted condemnation from some Extremely Concerned People. These individuals are more concerned about what you have failed to do for them (i.e., give them a baby) rather than they are concerned about you. Therefore, they go to the extreme to emphatically register their concern.

Of all the expressed concerns, none is more impactful to your personhood than the suggestion that your spouse should find another man or woman who would cause them to become a parent. That is such a formal accusation of one's humanity (your womanhood or your manhood). Do not forget those extreme parents and in-laws (especially some mothers and mothers-in-law), who demand a grandchild before they die, as if they have a fast-approaching date with death.

It usually starts out as a question: "When am I going to have a grandchild?"

Then it becomes a request: "Please give me a grandchild by my next birthday."

Next it progresses to a suggestion: "We think you should just go ahead and get pregnant and get it over with."

A short while after that, it matures into a full-fledged demand: "I want you to give me a grandchild. After all, every one of my other children who are married has given me grandchildren. Up until now, you would not even give me one. Look how long you have been married. At least, get pregnant." This is hilarious.

I sense your uneasiness at this point. Please, try not to get angry with these well-meaning people. They are just

Extremely Concerned Individuals who are looking out for you. Well, enough of the charade. If you ask me for my candid opinion, I think the whole progression reeks of selfishness at every level. The humblest of rationales, embraced by every one of the Extremely Concerned Individuals, expresses self-interest. None of the Extremely Concerned Individuals from your close circle of relatives and friends had given you a baby to keep, which should have been returned based on their expectations and timing. They do not have the faintest idea how hard you have been trying. Then, the greatest insult of all: they have the unbridled presumption and unmitigated gall to demand a grandchild and suggest that you have been cursed if you do not produce evidence of your fertility. A word of advice to all levels of Extremely Concerned Individuals: let people be and take your concerns to God. There is no need to call your daughter-in-law a witch. Avoid going to ritualists to request a spiritual cleansing of your in-law so that he or she can have a baby. Take the matter to God. He is the Baby Giver, the Pregnancy Keeper, and the Conception Igniter. Would-be parents, God knows that you are tired of hearing that Long playing (LP) record stuck on the track, "When Are You Going to Have a Baby?" It is time for a paradigm-shift – a change in thinking. A paradigm is a way of looking at something (i.e., a way of perceiving that thing, a perspective). When you change paradigms, you are changing how you think about something. So, leave the naysayers behind and launch out in faith. Get bold like

Hannah before you get old like Sarah. Partner with the Baby-Giver, the Pregnancy Keeper, and the Conception Igniter. Reach out like Hannah and God will come through for you. He always comes through. He did it instantly for the three Hebrew boys at the fiery furnace. He did it overnight for Daniel in the lion's den. He did it after three days for Mary and Martha when He raised Lazarus from the grave. He did it repeatedly for the four thousand and the five thousand hungry souls who Jesus fed. He can also do it for you. Just reach out to Him in faith, as Hannah did. That could be the spark that ignites a turn of events in your life. Ostensibly, this could be your turn.

CHAPTER 8

Your Turn Now—"Yes, You"

YOU MAY HAVE heard the saying, "There's a time for everything under the sun." Well, it is a paraphrasing of a Bible passage summarized in one sentence. Here is the actual Bible passage:

> To every thing there is a season,
> And a time to every purpose under the heaven:
> A time to be born, and a time to die;
> A time to plant, and a time to pluck up that which is planted; A time to kill, and a time to heal;
> A time to break down, and a time to build up;
> A time to weep, and a time to laugh;

A time to mourn, and a time to dance;

A time to cast away stones,

And a time to gather stones together;

A time to embrace, and a time to refrain from

embracing; A time to get, and a time to lose;

A time to keep, and a time to cast away;

A time to rend, and a time to sew;

A time to keep silence, and a time to speak;

A time to love, and a time to hate;

A time of war, and a time of peace. (Ecclesiastes

3:1–8, Authorized King James Version)

Therefore, based on God's word, there must be a time for your turn—your turn to have a baby, your turn to add the sound of little *pitter-patter* to your family. Consequently, I believe that now is the time for your turn. Even after diligently doing all that you know and yet that moment of annunciation of your desired conception has continued to elude you, I still declare that there is still a time for your turn. Just be aware that the time for your turn is based on God's *fullness of time.*

It is likely to believe that, if ever there were a husband and wife whose prayer would be answered quickly, that would be the parents of John the Baptist (Jesus's cousin). Here is how the Bible describes them:

> There was in the days of Herod, the king
> of Judaea, a certain priest named Zacharias,
> of the course of Abia: and his wife was of
> the daughters of Aaron, and her name
> was Elizabeth. And They Were Both
> Righteous Before God, Walking In All The
> Commandments And Ordinances Of The
> Lord Blameless. And They Had No Child,
> Because That Elisabeth Was Barren, And
> They Both Were Now Well Stricken In Years.
> (Luke 1:5–7, Authorized King James Version)

They were righteous and blameless in all things. That was their spiritual resume, based on God's assessment. If anyone could have gotten a prayer through to God, it would have been those two. Nevertheless, several years had passed, and the time for *their turn* to have a baby had not yet arrived. Something else was going on outside of their standing with God, and out of their control. The reason that many years of prayer for a child, by Zacharias and Elizabeth, had not been answered was because it was not yet time for God the Father to send Jesus (the Messiah) to this earth. The Bible informs us in Galatians 4:4–5 (KJV),

> But when the fullness of the time was come,
> God sent forth his Son, made of a woman,
> made under the law, to redeem them that

were under the law, that we might receive the adoption of sons. ... When the fullness of time was come God sent forth his son.

It was God's plan all along to choose the son of Zacharias and Elizabeth as the forerunner of the World's Redeemer. Therefore, exactly six months before the Messiah (Jesus) would be conceived, the forerunner (John the Baptist) needed to be conceived. Timing is of the essence with God. The good old Spiritual Song declares,

> He's an 'On Time' God. Yes, He is!
> He may not come when you want Him,
> But He'll be there right 'on time'.
> Oh, He's an 'On Time' God. Yes, He is!

The Holy Bible states in Luke 1:8–13 (KJV),

> And it came to pass, that while he executed the priest's office before God in the order of his course ... there appeared unto him an angel of the Lord standing on the right side of the altar of incense. And when Zacharias saw him, he was troubled, and fear fell upon him. But the angel said unto him, Fear not, Zacharias: for thy prayer is heard; and thy wife Elisabeth shall bear thee a son, and thou shalt call his name John.

When Elizabeth was six months pregnant, the same angel mentioned in (Luke 1:9, KJV), Gabriel, appeared to her young cousin Mary. This is so fantastic that it is too good for me to paraphrase. So here is the biblical account as the Holy Spirit gave it to the medical doctor and historian, Dr. Luke. "And after those days his wife Elisabeth Conceived, And Hid Herself Five Months, saying, Thus hath the Lord dealt with me in the days wherein he looked on me, to take away my reproach among men. And In The Sixth Month The Angel Gabriel Was Sent From God Unto A City Of Galilee, Named Nazareth, To A Virgin Espoused To A Man Whose Name Was Joseph, Of The House Of David; And The Virgin's Name Was Mary. And the angel came in unto her, and said, Hail, thou that art highly favoured, the Lord is with thee: blessed art thou among women. And when she saw him, she was troubled at his saying, and cast in her mind what manner of salutation this should be. And The Angel Said Unto Her, Fear Not, Mary: For Thou Hast Found Favour With God. And, Behold, Thou Shalt Conceive In Thy Womb, And Bring Forth A Son, And Shalt Call His Name Jesus. He shall be great, and shall be called the Son of the Highest: and the Lord God shall give unto him the throne of his father David: And he shall reign over the house of Jacob for ever; and of his kingdom there shall be no end. Then said Mary unto the angel, How shall this be, seeing I know not a man? And the angel answered and said unto her, The Holy Ghost shall come upon thee, and the power of the Highest shall overshadow thee: therefore also that holy thing which shall be born of thee shall be called the Son of God. And, Behold, Thy Cousin Elisabeth, She Hath Also Conceived A Son In Her Old Age: And This Is The Sixth Month With Her, Who Was Called Barren. For With God Nothing Shall Be Impossible. And Mary said, Behold the handmaid of the Lord; be it unto me according to thy word. And the angel departed from her. And Mary Arose In Those Days, And Went Into The Hill Country With Haste, Into A City Of Juda; And Entered Into The House Of Zacharias, And Saluted Elisabeth. And It Came To Pass, That, When Elisabeth Heard The Salutation Of Mary, The Babe Leaped In Her Womb; And Elisabeth Was Filled With The Holy Ghost: And She Spake Out With A Loud Voice, And Said, Blessed Art Thou Among Women, And Blessed Is The Fruit Of Thy Womb. And Whence Is This To Me, That The Mother Of My Lord Should Come To Me? For, Lo, As Soon As The Voice Of Thy Salutation Sounded In Mine Ears, The Babe Leaped in my womb for joy. And blessed is she that believed: for there shall be a performance of those things which were told her from the Lord. And Mary said, My soul doth magnify the Lord, And my spirit hath rejoiced in God my Saviour. For he hath regarded the low estate of his handmaiden: for, behold, from henceforth all generations shall call me blessed. For he that is mighty hath done to me great things; and holy is his name. And his mercy is on them that fear him from generation to generation. He hath shewed strength with his arm; he hath scattered the proud in the imagination of their hearts. He hath put down the mighty from their seats, and exalted them of low degree. He hath filled the hungry with good things; and the rich he hath sent empty away. He hath helped his servant Israel, in remembrance of his mercy; As he spake to our fathers, to Abraham, and to his seed for ever. And Mary Abode With Her About Three Months, And Returned To Her Own House." LUKE 1:24–56 (KJV)

Now, let's put it all together. Six months before the conception of the Messiah (Jesus) by his mother Mary, God blessed Mary's older and barren cousin, Elizabeth, with the conception of John the Baptist (the forerunner of the Messiah). That's right! Six months before the conception of Jesus, it was Elizabeth's turn to become pregnant. In the fullness of time (Galatians 4:4, KJV), God's time, it was Elizabeth's turn to become pregnant with that long-desired and prayed-for baby.

If God once worked one miracle, He could do it again. What He did for Elizabeth and Zacharias, He can also do for you. Before them, He had done it for Sarah and Abraham. He had done it for Jacob and Rachel. He had also done it for Hannah and Elkanah. Furthermore, there is an emphatic assurance that He'll do it for you, in the unwavering words of the Psalmist's positive affirmation: "He (GOD) makes the barren woman to keep house, and to be a joyful mother of children. Praise ye the Lord" (Psalm 113:9, KJV).

Praise the Lord! Hallelujah to the keeper of His word. Sarah had trusted God for a son, and three months later, it was her turn to become pregnant. Nine months after, she gave birth to Isaac, fulfilling the prophecy of God in Genesis 17:21 (KJV) that it would happen "at this set time in the next year."

After many years of anguish, it was Rachel's and Hannah's turn to have their babies. In God's fullness of time, they received their babies. In the fullness of time, it was Rachel's turn: "God remembered Rachel, and God hearkened to her, and opened her womb" (Genesis 30:22, KJV).

In the fullness of time, it was Hannah's turn: "And Elkanah knew Hannah his wife; and the Lord remembered her" (1 Samuel 1:19, KJV). In the fullness of time (not so long ago), it was our turn (my wife and I): "He maketh the barren woman to keep house, and to be a joyful mother of children. Praise ye the Lord" (Psalm 113:9, KJV).

Always remember that there is a time for everything under the sun, a time for trying various conjugal positions to enhance conception and a time for going with what is natural and comfortable. A time for copulating at specific times of the day to get that baby and a time for "any time of the day." A time for trusting in feng shui and a time to forget about feng shui. A time for using black cohosh, ashwagandha, capadulla, maca, moringa, sarsaparilla, licorice, locust bark, and yohimbe to improve the chances of pregnancy and a time for going without using any of them. A time for trying in vitro fertilization and a time for no in vitro fertilization. A time for using mandrakes to become pregnant and a time to become pregnant without the use of mandrakes. A time when it's other people's turn to have a baby and a time when it's your turn.

Dear readers of *When Mandrakes Don't Work*, only you and God hold the secret to that moment when it's *your turn* to have a baby.

CHAPTER 9

Beyond Mandrakes— Baby Syndrome

IN A HISTORIC address to the British Parliament on May 25, 2011, Barak Obama, former president of the United States, stated this observation, which is common to both the USA and the United Kingdom:

> Through the struggles of slaves and immigrants, women and ethnic minorities, former colonies and persecuted religions, we have learned better than most that the longing for freedom and human dignity is not English

or American or Western. It is universal and it
beats in every heart.

Today, I would like to make a personal observation:
through the struggles with contraception and abortion,
vasectomy and tubal ligation, miscarriages and premature
births, follicle stimulating hormone (FSH) drugs and Viagra,
in vitro fertilization, and surrogate mothering, I have realized
that the longing for motherhood and having one's own baby
is neither Asian nor African, Australian nor European, North
American nor South American, Islandic nor Continental. It
is universal, and it beats in every female's heart.

All around the world, while in the innocence of
childhood play, little girls begin to wonder and talk about
getting married and having a baby. Having a baby is common
talk for them while they play 'House' without any thought
of sexual interaction. Although they might not be able to
explain the origin of that first desire, it appears to be deeply
innate and prenatal. I hereby declare that this innate desire
to have a baby is nothing less than the classic display of a
Divinely Inspired Baby Syndrome (DIBS).

- Now inspiration is described as the process of being mentally stimulated to do or feel something—specially to do something creative.
- Medically, a syndrome is a group of symptoms which consistently occur together, or a condition that is characterized by a set of associated symptoms.
- Mentally, a syndrome is a characteristic combination of opinions, emotions, and behaviors.

As a result, I believe that this universal, innate desire to have a baby is prompted by divine inspiration by the God of Creation. Therefore, I submit to you that this Divinely Inspired Baby Syndrome (DIBS) is a mentality that was stimulated by the Creator God (Mankind's Creator) in the mind of every human female to conceive and give birth to a baby. DIBS is a common phenomenon resident (though latent) in every baby girl and boy. Men share the same desire about becoming a parent as their female counterparts. Although less expressed by some men and sometimes selectively suppressed by both men and women, the longing for parenthood is mutual. Yes, Divinely Inspired Baby Syndrome (DIBS) is universal, and it beats in every human heart. DIBS is a natural, healthy syndrome common to humanity. Long before the child is born, Divinely Inspired Baby Syndrome (DIBS) beats in the heart of every baby. When we consider DIBS in connection with God's command in Genesis 1:28 (KJV), to multiply and fill the earth, DIBS becomes an enabler for fulfilling that divine instruction. Simply put, Divinely Inspired Baby Syndrome (DIBS) constantly stimulates and motivates us to make babies and populate the earth. I now invite you to consider a little verse in Proverbs 20:18 (KJV), as it is given in three different versions of the Bible (*emphasis added*).

1. King James Version
   * Every *purpose* is established by *counsel*: and with good advice make war.
2. Revised Standard Version
   * *Plans* are established by *counsel*, by wise guidance wage war.
3. World English Bible
   * *Plans* are established by *advice*; by wise guidance you wage war!

From the correspondingly italicized words in each version, we see that *purpose* was replaced by *plans* and *counsel* was replaced by *advice*. Hence, if plans are established by advice, then advice is given for the purpose of fulfilling plans. Therefore, it is logical to conclude that God's advice to man—"make babies and fill the earth"—was given because God had a plan. So, I began investigating what exactly was God's plan when He counseled human beings in Genesis 1:28 (KJV) to "be fruitful, and multiply, and replenish [fill] the earth." What was the plan in the mind of God when He gave humankind the advice to make babies and fill the earth? After researching various Bible versions, renowned Bible commentaries, several theological research papers, and libraries of books, I discovered something I would like to share with you. I believe it gives us a revelation about God's mastermind plan behind advising mankind to fill the earth through the process of sexual reproduction. Let me share that treasure with you.

While highlighting "Legends of Faith" in Hebrews 11(KJV), the Word of God describes these "Legends of Faith" as pilgrims who expected a heavenly country. Then the Bible says emphatically that God had already prepared a city in heaven for them. Here are the exact words of the Holy Bible from the King James Version (KJV) and the New Living Translation (NLT) respectively:

> These all died in faith, not having received the promises, but having seen them afar off, and were persuaded of them, and embraced them, and confessed that they were strangers and pilgrims on the earth. For they that say such things declare plainly that they seek a country. And truly, if they had been mindful of that country from whence they came out, they might have had opportunity to have returned. But now they desire a better country, that is, an heavenly: wherefore God is not ashamed

to be called their God: *For He Hath Prepared For Them A City.* (Hebrews 11:13–16, KJV)

All these people died still believing what God had promised them. They did not receive what was promised, but they saw it all from a distance and welcomed it. They agreed that they were foreigners and nomads here on earth. Obviously, people who say such things are looking forward to a country they can call their own. If they had longed for the country they came from, they could have gone back. But they were looking for a better place, a heavenly homeland. That is why God is not ashamed to be called their God, *for he has prepared a city for them.* (Hebrews 11:13–16, NLT)

The last words of Hebrews 11:16 (KJV *emphasis added*), inform us that God had already prepared a city for all the faithful pilgrims, and they were looking forward to that heavenly homeland. Wow! Did you get that? Let me unpackage this gem of information in simpler terms. God prepared a city in heaven to be the final home for humanity. Then God promised humanity that if they were faithful to Him, the city in heaven would be their final home. As a result, they lived in joyful obedience to God, expecting the time when they would be at home with God in that heavenly city. Therefore, beginning from Abel in Hebrews 11:4 (KJV), to Sampson, David, Samuel, and the Prophets in Hebrews 11:32 (KJV), they all knew that God's plan was to add them to the angelic population of heaven.

One of the world's most famous authors, the most translated American nonfiction author of any era, whom *Smithsonian Magazine* named among the "100 Most Significant Americans of All Time," penned the following statements:

> God created man for his own glory, that after test and trial the human family might become one with the Heavenly family. It was God's purpose to repopulate Heaven with the Human family if they would show themselves obedient to his every word. Adam was to be tested, to see whether he would be obedient, as the loyal angels, or disobedient. (E. G. White, *God's Amazing Grace*)

> The vacancies made in Heaven by the fall of Satan and his angels will be filled by the redeemed of the Lord. (E.G. White, *The Truth about Angels*)

Today, this renowned Christian author's writings continue to influence millions of people worldwide. In this case, the words of the above extracts from her writings serve to echo the Truth of The Infallible Word of God (the Holy Bible).

Therefore, God commanded/advised human beings in Genesis 1:28 (KJV) to multiply babies and populate the earth, because God's ultimate plan was (and still is) to repopulate heaven with humanity as a replacement for Lucifer (Satan) and the other rebellious angels that were evicted from Heaven. As a result, mankind was created by God with a DNA-ingrained, prenatal Divinely Inspired Baby Syndrome (DIBS). That is why the longing for fatherhood, motherhood, and having one's own baby is not Asian nor African, Australian nor European, North American nor South American, Islandic nor Continental. It is universal, and it beats in every human heart. Divinely Inspired Baby Syndrome (DIBS) is universal. Before the use of mandrakes, humans were infused with this DIBS. In fact, I submit that it is because of this universal Divinely Inspired Baby Syndrome (DIBS) that people are driven to seek the use of mandrakes. Consequently, mandrakes or no mandrakes, while humans still have the splendor of time, mankind will always be stimulated by DIBS. Dear friends, and readers, beyond the quest for mandrakes; even "When Mandrakes Don't Work," DIBS will continue its universal work.

Printed in the United States
by Baker & Taylor Publisher Services